# I like school

## Bobbie Kalman

Toronto
New York
Crabtree Publishing Company

**The In My World Series**
Conceived and coordinated by Bobbie Kalman

**Writing team:**
Bobbie Kalman
Diane Cook-Brissenden
Susan Hughes

**Editors:**
Susan Hughes
Ruth Chernia

**Cover and title page design:**
Oksana Ruczenczyn, Leslie Smart and Associates

**Design and mechanicals:**
Ruth Chernia

**Illustrations:**
Title page by Karen Harrison © Crabtree Publishing Company 1985
Pages 28-32 by Deborah Drew-Brook-Cormack
© Crabtree Publishing Company 1985
Pages 4-27 and cover © Mitchell Beazley Publishers 1982

Cataloging in Publication Data

Kalman, Bobbie, 1947–
  I like school

(The In my world series)
ISBN 0-86505-064-3

1. School environment – Juvenile literature.
I. Title. II. Series.

LB1513.K34 1985          j372.1

**To Olivia**

350 Fifth Avenue
Suite 3308
New York, N.Y. 10118

102 Torbrick Avenue
Toronto, Ontario
Canada M4J 4Z5

# Contents

# I am in kindergarten

This is my first year at school.
I go to school all morning.
On the first morning, I was scared. I missed Mom.
Now I like school.
There are lots of fun things to do here.
We sing songs.
The teacher reads us books.
We draw pictures and make up stories.

I can play with all kinds of toys.
Sometimes I have to share the toys
with others, but I don't mind.
Now I have many friends.
I know my friends like playing with the toys too.

I still miss my mom sometimes, but
I like playing with my friends.

We are getting ready to go home now.
Some of my friends know how to
dress themselves.
I can tie up my laces.
I am doing more things by myself now that I am
in school, but I still need help doing up buttons.
My teacher helps me button up my coat.
Soon I will learn how to do up buttons by myself.

School is a place to learn new things.
School is a place to have fun.
I'm glad I am going to school.

## Picture talk

Did your life change when you started
going to school? How?
What new things have you learned to do
since you started school?

# I go to school all day

My name is Angela.
Last year I was in kindergarten.
I only went to school in the morning.
Now I am in first grade.
I go to school all day.
At first it was hard to be in school all day.
Now I like it.

I like my class because we have first
and second grade children in it.
My friend Paul is in second grade, but
he is in my classroom.

We have math and science in the morning.
We learn how to sort and measure things.
We count and learn to write numbers.
We learn reading and writing in the afternoon.
We sing songs and play music too.

Today Paul and I are learning how to use
the scales.
I am putting blocks on my side of the scales.
Paul is putting coloring pencils on his side.
My blocks are heavier than his pencils.

My teacher and my friend Bobbie are using
blocks to learn about numbers.
Soon my teacher will work with Paul and me.
She shows us how to learn things on our own.

## Picture talk

What do you most enjoy doing in school?
What work can you do on your own?
What do you find hard to do on your own?
Can you name the shapes and colors
in the border of this picture?

# I love science best!

Science is my favorite subject.
My teacher, Mr. Cormack, doesn't just use
books to teach us.
He brings animals, bugs, and other living
things right into the classroom.
Sometimes my class goes outside
to search for leaves and flowers.

We're learning about snails this week.
Snails are fun because they don't run from us.
Maybe they're just not afraid!
We watch them move slowly.
They always carry their houses on their backs.
Can you imagine carrying your home?

Today Mr. Cormack let us pretend to be snails.
We crawled from one side of the classroom
to the other with heavy knapsacks on our backs.
We got tired very quickly.
I guess we're not as strong as snails are.

Tomorrow our snails will have a race.
We will put leaves in the center of the room.
The snails will be placed so that they are each
the same distance from the leaves.
Then we will cheer our favorite snails
to victory.
What a fun way to learn about snails!

## Picture talk

Which snail do you think will win the race?
How are these children learning about snails?
What is the girl on the right looking through?
What is she looking at?

8

# Library time

The best part of school is learning to read.
I go to a small school.
My school does not have a library.
When we want to get books to read, my class
goes down the street to the public library.
I have my own library card.
I can take out any book I want.

Libraries are lots of fun.
They are full of secret treasures.
When I open a book, I might find an exciting
story, some beautiful drawings, or photographs
of children from other countries.
My favorite books are about dinosaurs.

My teacher goes to the library with my class.
She chooses books to read to us during the week.
My teacher likes funny books.
We all laugh when she reads to us.

The library has special rules.
We must speak quietly when we are there.
People like to read in a quiet place.
We must not write in library books.
We have to return the books we borrow.
Sometimes I find a book in the back of my desk.
It is overdue.
I must pay a fine when I take the book
back to the library.
The fine helps me remember to return
my book on time the next time!

**Picture talk**

Do you have a library at your school?
When do you use it?
What are your favorite books about?

# Making music

My name is Ricky.
This is my music class.
Can you see me playing the recorder?
Watch my fingers fly!

Mr. Sandburg is our music teacher.
He shows us how to play the instruments.
1—2—3—4. We are following the rhythm.
Yoli and Tibor are playing the drums.
Mark and Marie are playing the tambourine
and the triangle.
Pam and Mike are playing xylophones.
Karl and Eva are shaking maracas.
The rest of my friends are playing recorders.

We sing songs from all over the world.
When Mr. Sandburg plays the piano or guitar,
we follow the tune.
I can make my voice sing a high note.
I can make my voice sing a low note.

I like singing, but I like playing
the recorder even better.
I would like to play the flute,
but first I must learn to read music.
Maybe one day I can play in the school band.

## Picture talk

How many shaking instruments do you see
in the picture and the border?
Which instruments make a sound
when air is blown into them?
Which instruments must be strummed or plucked?
Which instruments have to be tapped or hit?
Which instrument would you like to play?

## It's recess

Ralph is my name. Soccer is my game.
I learned to play soccer at school during
my physical education class.
I like to play soccer during recess.

I'm Peter. I am new at this school.
I could skip with my own rope,
but I don't want to.
I would rather play with the other children,
but they didn't ask me to play with them.
I know school is a good place to
make friends, but I'm too shy to tell the kids
that I want to play with them.

I'm Tina. I am waiting for my turn at marbles.
I did not always wait for my turn.
I used to get impatient.
The other kids got angry with me.
I have learned to wait for my turn.
Now my friends and I have fun
when we play marbles.

I'm Elaine. I like recess.
I like to run and jump.
I like to spin and skip.
I'm glad we have recess twice a day!

### Picture talk

If you were skipping, would you ask Peter
to join your game?
How would you ask him?
Which children are waiting for a turn?
Why do people have to take turns?
Playing with friends is fun. Playing alone
is also fun. What games do you play by yourself?

# My imagination

My imagination makes learning fun.
I can become an animal just as easy as this.
Stomp! Stomp! Stomp!
I can make my body feel heavy.
I am a huge gray elephant with big ears.

I can make my body feel light.
I can pretend to swing and climb and hang.
Now I am a monkey.

I can pretend to glide through the air.
I can stand in the water on one leg.
Did you guess?
I am a pink flamingo.

I use my imagination in other ways too.
Sometimes I pretend I am grown up.
I use my imagination when I draw pictures
or write stories.
My teacher puts a gold star on my work.
She thinks my stories are very good.

My teacher says that having a good
imagination is just as important as being
good at math or reading.
I am glad because I have a great imagination!

## Picture talk

Which animals are the children pretending to be?
Which animals can you see on
the classroom walls?
What animals are the children drawing?
How is the boy with the broken arm
using his imagination?
How do you use your imagination?

## What is art?

Why are we wearing shirts to cover our clothes?
Why are our hands different colors?
When we create, we get messy!

My favorite activity at school is art.
Art is painting. Art is molding.
Art is building. Art is drawing.
Art is making something that is special to me.
I like art because it helps me to show
my ideas.

Nina is making a face.
She presses her fingers into the clay to mold
a mouth and face.
The clay feels squishy!
Jennifer and Amy are building a crocodile.
Have you ever seen such a creature?

I am painting with my fingers.
Morgan is painting with a brush.
Hands, feet, potatoes, and fruit
all become pictures when I dip them
into paint and press them onto paper.

The finished paintings are put on the wall.
I hope the teacher puts up my painting!

### Picture talk

What materials are the children using to make
the crocodile?
Which art activity would you choose to do? Why?
Which is your favorite way of painting?
How are some of the children cleaning up?
Why is it important to help clean up?

# Field day

We have a physical education class
three times a week.
We run, play games, and do exercises
to music.

Twice a year we have a track and field day
at school.
Everyone in the school goes outside.
We run and jump and throw.
We cheer for one another.

I can run faster and jump farther
this year than I could last year.
I used to cry if I didn't win a race.
Now I don't cry when I lose.
I know I can't win all the time.
I feel good as long as I know
I have tried my best.

My friend Otto is in a wheelchair.
He can't run, but he is learning
to throw the discus.
The coach is teaching Otto exercises
to strengthen the muscles in his arms.

My friend Marie is doing a long jump.
She flies through the air and lands in the sand.
She has been practicing all week.
How far did she jump?

## Picture talk

Do you have a field day at your school?
Which is your best sport?
Do you think it is important
to win a race? Why or why not?

# Outdoor education

My class went on a hike for the day. ·
Our teacher and four parents took us to a park.
We walked along trails in the woods.
We saw small animals and many kinds of birds.
We collected leaves of different colors.

We made a path across the stream.
We used stones and logs.
Ed brought his dog Rocky on the hike.
Rocky didn't use our stones and logs
to cross the stream!

We were very hungry after all the exercise.
We learned to make a campfire and then had
a cook-out lunch. It tasted great.

The walk back seemed long.
We were all very tired,
but we sang all the way home.

I can't wait until next year.
Next year my class will go on
an overnight camping trip.
We will learn about trees and lakes,
rivers and streams.
My school calls it Outdoor Education.
I think that outdoor education is the best way
to learn about nature.

## Picture talk

What season of the year is it? How do you know?
Could these children use stepping stones
to cross deep water?
How have the children made sure their campfire
will not spread?

# A trip to the museum

I am always getting into trouble.
I don't try to. It just happens.

Today my class went to the museum.
First we looked at the beetle display.
Then we looked at the mummies all wrapped up.
We saw china dolls, and toys of long ago.
I liked the beetles, the mummies, the dolls, and
the toys, but I could not wait to see the
dinosaur skeletons.
My teacher kept saying, "Wait a little longer,
Charles. We will be seeing the dinosaurs soon."

Just then, I peeked into the next room
and there it was, the brontosaurus,
my favorite dinosaur.
I was so excited.
I couldn't stop myself. I couldn't wait.
I ran into the next room.
Right in front of me was the enormous tail
of the great brontosaurus.
It was so big, I had to jump up to touch it.
I imagined myself riding through jungles
on the back of the brontosaurus.
I imagined adventures we could have.

Then I saw the museum guard and my teacher
coming toward me.
I remembered where I was and I knew
I was in trouble again!
Why does it always happen to me?

## Picture talk

Why should you not touch exhibits at a museum?
Why do you think Charles gets into trouble?
Do you get into trouble sometimes?

# After school

I'm Nathan.
When school gets out, my friend
Mona goes home.
Daniel goes to his grandmother's house.
I go to my day-care center.
My mommy and daddy work in a
big office downtown.
They can't pick me up until 6 o'clock.

Most of the time, I like being at day care.
When I arrive at the center, I have a snack
so I won't be hungry before dinner.
I play with other kids.
We make things at the art table.
We build things at the block center.
We pretend at the dress-up center.
Sometimes I like to be by myself,
so I choose something quiet to do.
I go to the reading center or the
listening center.

There are many things to do
at day care, but I am always ready to
go home at the end of the day.
I am always happy to see my mom and dad.

### Picture talk

Where do you go after school?
What do you do there?
Look at all the activities in the picture.
Which one would you choose to do? Why?
Do you ever like to be alone? When?
What do you like to do when you are alone?
Where would you go if you were at this
day-care center and wanted to be alone?

26

## A school day

Was it hard for you to get used to a whole day at school? Did you get hungry before lunchtime? Did you get tired before the school day ended? What other things did you find hard to get used to? What would you do if the following things happened to you?

1.  You are sitting at your desk and suddenly you feel very sick. Your teacher is busy with one of the reading groups. What should you do?

2.  You go outside for recess. One of the kids in grade five calls you names. What can you do?

3.  You and your friend have been talking. Your teacher tells you to be quiet. You go back to work but your friend keeps talking to you. What would you do?

4.  You have been working hard on a picture for art. You think it is special. You are almost finished when one of your classmates comes up to you and tells you that your picture is stupid. What would you do?

## Willie wants to stay home

My mom wakes me every morning at 7 o'clock.
"Time to get up for school, Willie," she calls.
Well, today I'm not going to school. I told her so.
"What do you mean you're not going to school?
You have to go to school, Willie," Mom says.
"But Mom," I said, "you don't go to work every day.
Why do I have to go to school every day?"

It's not that I don't like school.
I just don't like to go to school *every* day.
And I don't like to go *all* day.
My stomach growls for food long before
I get to eat lunch.
I like my teacher, but there are so many kids
in my class that sometimes I think
my teacher forgets about me.
I like to learn, but I can't sit at my
desk for such a long time.

Recess is my favorite part of the day.
Well, it *was* my favorite part until this big kid
from the fourth grade came along.
Whenever he sees me, he says, "Oh look,
there's Willie Nillie."
"My name is not Willie Nillie," I tell him.
"It's Willie, just plain old Willie!"
But he only looks at me with a funny grin
and goes on calling, "Willie Nillie, Willie Nillie,
Willie Nillie," until I want to scream.

As I sit at the table eating my corn flakes
with bananas on top, I remember that today is
my show-and-tell day.
I was going to bring a picture of my
new two-wheeler bicycle.
I also remember that today is the day
we're going to make dinosaurs out of clay.
I was going to make a tyrannosaurus rex.
And today is also the day I promised to play
with Leah and Jeremy at recess.
Maybe I will go to school after all.
I can always stay home tomorrow.

**Later that morning . . .**
When Mom dropped me off at school,
I lined up with the other kids.
My teacher came out to meet our class.
She looked right at me and gave me a wink!
I guess I am glad I came to school.
I think I'll probably come tomorrow.

# Recess games
## Duck, Duck, Goose

Form a circle with your friends. Hold hands. One of you is IT. That person must walk around the outside of the circle. He or she taps each friend's head, saying, "Duck, Duck, Duck . . ."

Finally, IT taps a friend's head and says, "Goose." Goose runs around the outside of the circle. IT runs in the other direction. The first one back to Goose's place in the circle may remain there. The other person will now be IT.

## Fox and Geese

Clear a big circle in the snow with your feet. Clear six or eight lines going into the center of the circle. The snow design should look like a wheel with spokes. The person chosen to be Fox stands at the very center of the circle. The Geese run in one direction around the outside ring. Fox then chases the Geese by running down the paths which go from the center to the outside. The Goose that is caught becomes the new Fox.

# Rainy day games
## "Um"

One player is blindfolded. The other players sit on the floor in a circle or half circle. The blindfolded player plunks down in front of another player, and says, "Um." The seated player says, "Um" three times in a disguised voice. The blindfolded player may not touch the seated player. She must guess who the person sitting in front of her is by listening to that person's voice.

If the blindfolded player guesses correctly, the blindfold is passed on to another player. All the other players change places and the game begins again. If the player who is IT does not guess correctly, she sits in front of a different child and tries again.

## Who's Missing?

Choose one person to be IT. The other players put down their heads and cover their eyes. The player who is IT very quietly taps someone on the head, who then leaves the room. IT says, "1—2—3, heads up." The children must try to guess who is hiding. When they guess correctly, the person who left the room becomes IT.

## -Up

even children are chosen to be IT. The other players ut their heads down and cover their eyes. Each of the hildren who are IT taps a player on the shoulder. he children who have been tapped put a humb up, but keep their heads down. The seven hildren who are IT go back to the front of the room. hey say, "7-Up." The players lift their heads. The even children who were tapped on the shoulder stand p. They each try to guess who tapped them. If a child uesses the right person, the children exchange places.

When all seven children have had a turn to guess, the ame starts again. If a child does not guess the right erson, a new child should be chosen to be IT.

## Stoneface

All the players sit in a circle. Each player has three small pebbles or stones. The first player begins the game by trying to make the person sitting next to him laugh or smile. He can make funny faces or tell silly jokes, but no touching or tickling is allowed.

If the person laughs before two minutes is up, she must put one of her pebbles into the center of the circle. Then it is her turn to try to make the person sitting next to her laugh or smile.

The game continues until only one person is left with any pebbles. The winner is called Stoneface. Can you guess why?

# Your Story

## Word helpers

These words will help you to write your own story about your school.

**school words**
kindergarten
grade
class
reading
writing
math
science
music
field trip
library
museum
field day
outdoor education
lunch
recess

**classroom words**
ruler
pencil
blackboard
table
center
desk
teacher
student
eraser
book

**art words**
painting
molding
drawing
building
clay
paint
crayon
paper
cardboard
smock
brush
glue
scissors

**action words**
draw
learn
jump
skip
play
paint
mold
build
measure
count
race

23456789 BP Printed in Canada 432109876